SECURE YOUR
LEGACY

ALL RIGHTS RESERVED. No part of this publication may be reproduced, distributed, or transmitted in any form or by any means, including photocopying, recording, or other electronic or mechanical methods, without the prior written permission of the publisher.

Published By: Pen Legacy, LLC.

DISCLAIMER AND/OR LEGAL NOTICES

The information contained within this Book is strictly for educational purposes. If you wish to apply ideas contained in this Book, you are taking full responsibility for your actions.

PRINTED IN THE UNITED STATES OF AMERICA

ISBN: 978-0996188043

All Rights Reserved. Copyright 2018

Pen Legacy LLC.

First Edition

Also by Charron Monaye

BOOKS

2018 Legacy Journal & Planner: A Planning Tool for your Freedom &; Future

I Matter Journal

STOP Asking for Permission &; Give Notice: How To Accept &; Attain Who You Are Without Validation

Love The Real You: Uncovering your "WHY" & Affirming You're Enough

UnBreak My Heart: From Scorn to Finding Love Again

My Side of the Story: From a Woman Waiting to Exhale

Fear Is A Crime: How To Overcome Fear & Face Your Destiny

I Want To Quit My Job: 8 Entrepreneurial Strategies for Massive Results While Employed

STAGE PLAYS

Get Out of Your Own Way

Why Can't We Be Friends

Living Your Life

Books are available on Amazon, Barnes N Noble, Books A Million, Wal-Mart

This Journal Belongs To:

_____

PEN LEGACY

DECLARTION OF PERSONAL FREEDOM & LEGACY

_____, from this day forward confess my commitment to myself, my dreams, my goals, and stay the course to my personal freedom and legacy. I will not allow anyone, including myself to keep me from living the life I want.

I AM committed to doing the work on myself so that I can enjoy and live to my fullest potential and be remembered for my offerings, love, and greatest qualities. I pledge:

1. To be honest with myself throughout this process.
2. To gain clarity of who I am so that I can be clear on what I want and how I need to receive it.
3. To engage with *only* positive and life-minded individuals that will provide support during this journey.
4. To attend at least one empowerment and financial workshop
5. To obtain a life coach or accountability partner to help you stay on course
6. To save 10% and invest 15% of my income.
7. To teach my children and share with my spouse any new discoveries or lessons learned.

I AM committed to this unwavering and personal covenant.

DATE: _____

PRINT NAME:

_____

SIGN NAME:

_____

Make It!

Manage It!

Multiply It!,

6 Awareness Questions To Prosperity

When you look at your life, how are you holding it? (Perspective)
_____
_____
_____
_____
_____
_____
_____
_____

Who are you "being" right now?
_____
_____
_____
_____
_____
_____
_____
_____

What are you Producing in this world?
_____
_____
_____
_____
_____
_____

What is your worth?

What is your secret power?

Tips To Manifesting Wealth

- Live Today as if you are living the life you want
- Speak what you want into existence.
- Live in your dream, not your reality.
- Live Life as if you already received it.
- You much compound Money to build Wealth.
- Without Peace you cannot create with clarity.
- Be completely unbothered by reality
- Stop operating in gifts that don't belong to you.

Types of Income

Earned Income

Earned income is money earned from working that requires your time. This is the income you receive from actively working. You work, and you are paid for your work.

Types
- Employment
- Small Business
- Consulting
- Gambling

Portfolio Income

Portfolio income is money you receive from selling an investment for more than what you paid for it (portfolio income is also referred to as capital gains).

Types:
- Trading (buying/selling) Paper Assets
    - Paper assets refer to things like stocks, bonds, mutual funds, ETFs, CDs, T-bills, currencies or other types of futures/derivatives.
    - Stock market investing is the most common generator of portfolio income
- Buying and Selling Real Estate
- Buying and Selling of Assets — Antiques or cars

Passive Income

Passive income is money generated from assets you own, where you are not actively working. Passive income is thought to be the key to building wealth. Once you have an investment that generates recurring income, you don't have to do much to maintain it.

Types:

- Interest – from a variety of loans, either to individuals (peer to peer lending or private notes) or companies (bonds, notes)
- Dividends – from investments, partnerships
- Capital gains – from the sale of investments
- Royalties – from products you sell or license
- Rental income – from real estate
- Business income – which may or may not be passive but the idea is you build something that generates income without active work, like a website or the sale of information products

6 Money Tips for a Wealthy Life!

- Money tip #1: Eliminate your debt
- Money tip #2: Invest in a 401k
- Money tip #3: Invest in a Roth IRA
- Money tip #4: Automate your finances
- Money tip #5: Leverage sub-savings accounts
- Money tip #6: Use target-date funds

10 Ways To Get Out of Debt

It's amazing that it's so easy (and often fun) to get into debt, but painfully difficult to get back out. It can take just a few months to create tens of thousands of dollars in debt, but sometimes decades to pay it off. Everyone who pays off their debt does it a different way and often combine strategies to knock out bad debt. Here are some ways to get out of debt.

- Stop Creating More Debt
- Increase Your Monthly Payment
- Build an Emergency Fund
- Pick One Debt and Give It All You've Got
- Ask Your Creditor for a Lower Interest Rate
- Look for Ways to Put More Money Towards Your Debt
- Withdraw From Your Retirement Fund
- Cash out a Life Insurance Policy
- Settle With Your Creditors
- Go Through Credit Counseling

PLAN + PREPARE = PROSPER

5 YEAR GOALS

1 YEAR GOAL

_____
_____
_____
_____
_____
_____
_____
_____
_____
_____
_____
_____
_____
_____
_____
_____
_____
_____
_____
_____
_____
_____

QUARTERLY GOALS

WEEKLY GOALS

LEGACY PLANNING LIST

WHAT IS YOUR LEGACY?

WHAT DO YOU WANT TO BE REMEMBERED FOR?

Fast forward to the end of your days, imagine you are on your death bed. When you look back on the life you have lived, what do you want to see? Answer the questions below, and if your answers do not align with the life you're living now, make some notes on the next few pages on how you need to change.

Do you want to see the life that was carefully designed and lived to the full extent or a life that just happened?

What kind of a family did you nurture? What do your family members think of you? What do they remember the most about you?

_____
_____
_____
_____
_____
_____
_____
_____
_____
_____
_____
_____
_____
_____
_____
_____
_____
_____
_____
_____
_____
_____

What kind of contribution would you have made to your community and society? Are you satisfied with the donations you made to charities?

What kind of values would you have cultivated and lived by?

How many friends would you have made? Are you proud of your friends and their achievements? How would they remember you?

Would the people be quoting your life as an example to follow?

Finally, if you had the opportunity to live again, would the life you just lived be an inspiration and an example for your new life?

_____
_____
_____
_____
_____
_____
_____
_____
_____
_____
_____
_____
_____
_____
_____
_____
_____
_____
_____
_____
_____
_____
_____

MY PERSONAL VISION STATEMENT IS....

Having a personal vision statement will allow you to aim in the desired direction both personally and professionally. Your vision should get you excited, make you proud, and illuminate where you are part of something bigger than yourself.

Example: "To inspire, motivate, and empower people to discover their life purpose and to reach their full potential."

_____
_____
_____
_____
_____
_____
_____
_____
_____
_____
_____
_____
_____
_____
_____

MY PERSONAL MISSION STATEMENT IS....

Your mission statement helps define what you do and helps to explain your purpose. It's the "why" of you. To create your personal mission statement, ask yourself when you are at your best, and when you are at your worst.

Example: To realize my vision, I must exceed the expectations of my friends, family, and readers. I will accomplish this by committing to my values and creativity, and by aiming for, and offering to others, the highest levels of creativity, spirituality, and information of which I am capable. I will maintain a focus on the value of creative freedom and the expression of that freedom which is most appropriate for each person. In this way I will help ensure that I honor my values, that what I offer is creatively innovative, and that my own growth goals are met along with the growth goals of those I come in contact with.

_____
_____
_____
_____
_____
_____
_____
_____
_____

I CHERISH THESE 8 THINGS THE MOST

1. _____

2. _____

3. _____

4. _____

5. _____

6. _____

7. _____

8. _____

IT'S TIME TO UNCOVER WHO YOU ARE?

WHO ARE YOU?

_____
_____
_____
_____
_____
_____
_____
_____
_____
_____
_____
_____
_____
_____
_____
_____
_____
_____
_____
_____
_____
_____
_____
_____
_____
_____
_____

WHO DOES YOUR FAMILY/CHILDREN/SPOUSE NEED YOU TO BE?

WHO DO YOU WANT TO BECOME?

TRAITS I DISLIKE ABOUT MYSELF

MY STRENGTHS ARE……

MY WEAKNESSES ARE…..

WHAT CHALLENGES AM I CURRENTLY FACING?

HOW DO I FEEL RIGHT NOW ABOUT MY LIFE?

IF I COULD CHANGE 8 THINGS ABOUT MYSELF WHAT WOULD THEY BE?

WHAT MAKES ME STAND OUT?

AM I IN MY OWN WAY? IF YES, HOW...

HAVE I REACH MY FULLEST POTENTIAL?
NO, WHY?

WHY AM I SO COMFORTABLE IN LIFE?

WHAT AM I AFRAID OF?

WHAT PAST HURT AM I HOLDING ON TO?

WHAT WOULD I NEED TO HAPPEN BEFORE I AM ABLE TO LET IT GO?

DO I LOVE MYSELF UNCONDITIONALLY? IN WHAT WAYS DO I SHOW MYSELF?

I DO THESE THINGS DAILY TO MAINTAIN SELF-LOVE?

1. _____

2. _____

3. _____

4. _____

5. _____

6. _____

I EMBRACE EVERYTHING ABOUT MYSELF, BUT.....

OBTAINING FREEDOM AND PEACE MEANS THIS TO ME.

BE HONEST HERE! THIS IS YOUR MOMENT OF DECLARING YOUR NEXT STEP

_____
_____
_____
_____
_____
_____
_____
_____
_____
_____
_____
_____
_____
_____
_____
_____
_____
_____
_____
_____
_____
_____

WHAT PEOPLE THINK ABOUT ME MATTERS? WHY

"I AM"

"I am" is one of the most powerful statements we can make.

Whatever follows "I am" starts the creation of it.

"I AM" AFFIRMATIONS

Decide now that this day is YOUR opportunity to turn things around for the better

I AM strong and balanced.

I AM much stronger and powerful than any challenge – I choose now to connect with that power.

I AM unstoppable

I AM brimming with energy

I AM always protected by my higher self

I AM grateful for the sense of well-being that fills my consciousness every day.

I AM now breathing deeply to elevate my mood and energize my body.

I AM Divine intelligence

I AM Love

I AM a part of something much bigger than myself. I choose to show up in my life and honor the opportunity that I have been given.

I AM flexible to changes happening in my life. The more accepting I am of change, the easier it feels. Change is a natural aspect of life. It is a sign of growth.

I AM open and allowing for positive things to unfold

I AM deserving

I AM willing to forgive so that I free myself from the chains of the past. I am freeing myself right now.

I AM proud of being unique. I am the only person on this planet with my fingerprints. I am me. There is only one me. I choose to honor that brilliant truth

I AM courageous and I stand up for myself – because I choose to be me

I AM now committed to take full responsibility for all my thoughts, actions and experiences. I can not change others. How I react to events are my responsibility, and that is brilliant, because I can choose to feel good whatever the circumstance.

I AM the master of my thoughts.

I AM willing to create new habits that support my personal growth

I am willing to accept the things I cannot change and allowing strength and courage into my life.

I AM choose to believe that everything that is happening now is happening for my ultimate good.

I AM now allowing myself to be totally in sync with life. Everything that happens has a deeper meaning.

MY PERSONAL "I AM" AFFIRMATIONS

I AM _____

_____

I AM _____

_____

I AM _____

_____

I AM _____

_____

I AM _____

_____

I AM _____

_____

I AM _____

_____

I AM _____

_____

I AM _____

_____

I AM _____

_____

I AM _____

_____

I AM _____

_____

I AM _____

_____

I AM _____

_____

I AM _____

_____

I AM _____

_____

I AM _____

_____

PERSONAL GOALS

HOW ARE YOU CHANGING THE GAME?

MY BUCKET LIST IS …..

GIVE EACH ITEM A DEADLINE TO COMPLETE.

I WANT TO TRAVEL TO THESE PLACES

I WANT TO EXPERIENCE THESE THINGS WITHIN THE END OF THIS YEAR

1. ⎯⎯⎯⎯⎯⎯⎯⎯⎯⎯⎯⎯⎯⎯⎯⎯⎯⎯⎯⎯⎯⎯⎯⎯⎯⎯⎯⎯

2. ⎯⎯⎯⎯⎯⎯⎯⎯⎯⎯⎯⎯⎯⎯⎯⎯⎯⎯⎯⎯⎯⎯⎯⎯⎯⎯⎯⎯

3. ⎯⎯⎯⎯⎯⎯⎯⎯⎯⎯⎯⎯⎯⎯⎯⎯⎯⎯⎯⎯⎯⎯⎯⎯⎯⎯⎯⎯

4. ⎯⎯⎯⎯⎯⎯⎯⎯⎯⎯⎯⎯⎯⎯⎯⎯⎯⎯⎯⎯⎯⎯⎯⎯⎯⎯⎯⎯

5. ⎯⎯⎯⎯⎯⎯⎯⎯⎯⎯⎯⎯⎯⎯⎯⎯⎯⎯⎯⎯⎯⎯⎯⎯⎯⎯⎯⎯

6. ⎯⎯⎯⎯⎯⎯⎯⎯⎯⎯⎯⎯⎯⎯⎯⎯⎯⎯⎯⎯⎯⎯⎯⎯⎯⎯⎯⎯

Do You Have A Story to Tell???

7 Steps to Consider Before Publishing Your Book

Pen Legacy Publishing, established in 2015 by Charron Monaye has become one of the most respected independent publishers amongst authors and readers. We pride ourselves on being the home for first-time writers and aspiring authors, as well as seasoned writers. Pen Legacy offers a variety of literature including, Non-Fiction, Contemporary Fiction, Inspirational/Self-Help, Autobiographies, Compilations and a host of other Fiction categories.

Charon Monye is an award-winning thought leader and prolific writer who started her writing career in 1994 when she contributed to the book anthology, Tears of Fire at the age of 14. Since then, Charron Monaye has been recognized as a Literary Game Changer who doesn't mind adapting words into legacies. She's been awarded Best Independent Author, authored 10 books, co-authored 4, published over 25 new authors, written/produced 3 theatrical productions, contributed to more than 20 book anthologies worldwide, and hired to pen other theatrical scripts such as; Testify, Til Death Do us Part, Oliva Lost & Turned Out, just to name a few.

Charron was formerly a staff writer for the Philadelphia Association of Paralegals, CNN iReport, and currently serves as a staff writer for the Department of Veteran Affairs, GovLoop.com, and Editor-In-Chief for www.madisonjaye.com. And is preparing to produce her first film, which started out as a book and later adapted into a theatrical production, "Get Out Of Your Own Way".

Now you see, I did not put that there to brag, but to let you know that the information within this section is real-life knowledge that I have learned throughout my career as a writer. Some people think publishing and being an author is easy, simply because they have Createspace, Kindle Direct Publishing, Lulu, Author House, Xlibris, and the other companies that make publishing easy. However, can I share a little secret with you? The true art of authorship does not start until you actually publish the book! The goal of any author or writer is to get their story out to the masses, but the types of publishing and the amount of knowledge you know about the industry will dictate how successful you are.

There are levels to publishing and before you hit the pay button, here are 7 steps to make sure that your manuscript is worth the investment.

- Make sure your manuscript is consistent in font and font size.
- Make sure your storyline is relevant and relatable.
- Make sure your manuscript is professional edited, at least 3 to 5 times. Covering all elements of editing:
    - Substantive editing
    - Copyediting
    - Proofreading
- Make sure you have a vibrant and storytelling book cover
- Make sure your synopsis matches the story plot or message that you are trying to convey.
- Make sure you know how to effectively price your book.
- Make sure you have a target audience follower, or support before you publish your book, there is nothing worse than to have a case of book and no sales.

If you need help before you pay to publishing, visit http://www.charronmonaye.com/coaching/

3 Avenues To Publishing

Trade or Traditional Publishers

Traditional publishing refers to the established system of getting a book deal, which involves submission to agents over a period of time, usually a number of rejections and then (hopefully) being accepted. Then the agent will submit the manuscript to publishers with usually a number of rejections and then (hopefully) a contract is signed. The book will then go through more edits and will eventually be published.

Vanity, Self and Contract Publishers

Vanity and contract presses print books under specialty contracts. Individual authors and companies pay all fees and costs for the publications printed in this category. These publishers assist in self-published books and charge fees based on the physical qualities of the book, including the number of pages and photographs, quality of the materials and the type of binding. The term vanity refers to the self-interest involved in the printing project. Small businesses interested in publishing firm histories, founder biographies and texts focusing on company products use this category of publishing press.

Electronic Books

Electronic book publishing offers readers the opportunity to download text online or purchase digital books from retail stores. " Only 6.2 percent of this total involved ebooks, but industry officials predict increased sales for digital books with huge increases for textbooks and best-selling trade books. Ebooks offer an inexpensive alternative for business-oriented publications and small printers interested in partnerships with large publishers operating networks to promote the ebooks.

Pros's and Con's of Traditional vs. Self-Publishing

PROS

The pros of traditional publishing
- Prestige, kudos and validation.
- Print distribution in bookstores is easier.
- An established professional team to work with.
- There are no upfront financial costs, and there's usually some kind of advance against royalties.
- Literary prizes and critical acclaim are more likely through traditional publishing,
- Potential to become a brand-name author.

The pros of being an indie author
- Total creative control over content and design.
- Sense of Accomplishment
- Faster time to market.
- Higher royalties.
- Sell by any means in any global market, as you retain the rights.

CONS

The cons of traditional publishing
- Incredibly slow process.
- Loss of creative control.
- Low royalty rates.
- Lack of significant marketing help.
- Once you sign a contract for your book, it essentially belongs to the publisher,

The pros of traditional publishing
- You need to do it all yourself or find suitable professionals to help.

- There's no prestige, kudos or validation by the industry.
- You need a budget upfront if you want a professional result.
- It's difficult to get print distribution in bookstores.
- Most literary prizes don't accept indie books
- The important thing is that you, the creator, are empowered to choose per project how you would like to progress.

Are you ready to Adapt Your Story into Script?
6 Easy Steps to Script Writing

It's always a blessing and a curse to see a great book turned into a movie. Most film adaptations never compare to their book predecessors, yet there's still the thrill of seeing the same story play out in two wildly different versions. And, of course, it's nice to know a story before you see a movie.

Have you seen movies such as The Hate You Give, A Wrinkle in Time, Ready Player One, The Secret Life of Bees, The Devil Wears Prada, Hannibal, Nappily Ever After, The Notebook, and Roots? The one thing they have in common is, they are all films that are also books. The one thing that makes books to script so appealing is the marketing strategy that is connected. When you think of Hollywood or "Major" Companies, we think of companies that want the character or the product established. Meaning you have to come to the table with a following, a plan, a pitch and a budget. Some want you to come with a ready script and film footage. But how do you do that if you don't have access, resources, or even a script. Well, in this section, I will focus on how to adapt your book to script, (screen or play). To learn the rest, visit my website for coaching, but here are a few steps.

1. Read books to learn how to write a script.
2. Read screenplays by some of your favorite movies/shows or that is related to your genre to learn the structure, flow and/or dynamics.
3. Outline some movies that you watch and pinpoint screenplay structure.
4. Outline your novel and find one storyline in the book that is relatable, timely, and entertaining.
5. Figure out your book's conflict! What's the core conflict that's going to make people pay money to want to go and see

it? Ask yourself some key questions and jot down notes on elements, like:
- Who's the protagonist?
- What's their goal?
- Who or what is the force of antagonism stopping them achieving this goal?
- Who or what's at stake if the protagonist doesn't achieve their goal?

6. Finalize your Outline & Start Writing Your Script

Writing Your Story

How Do I Get Started?

Do you know how many people come up to me at events, or for coaching saying, "I want to write a book, but don't know where to start". And my reply, is always, "get a book and pen then just write". I never understood why people think that there is a formula or some kind of written rule when it comes to writing. Once you know what you want to write about, the next step is to write.

So if you are one of those persons who want to write a book, but don't know where to start, here are a few steps to consider.

1. Decide what the book is about ~ Think of your book in terms of beginning, middle, and end. Anything more complicated will get you lost.

2. Set a daily word count goal ~ A page a day is only about 300 words. You don't need to write a lot. You just need to write often. Setting a daily goal will give you something to aim for. Make it small and attainable so that you can hit your goal each day and start building momentum.

3. Set a time to work on your book every day ~ Consistency makes creativity easier. You need a daily deadline to do your work — that's how you'll finish writing a book.

4. Write in the same place every time ~ Make your writing location a special space, so that when you enter it, you're ready to work. It should remind you of your commitment to finish this book.

5. Set a total word count ~ Begin with the end in mind. Once you've started writing, you need a total word count for your book. Think in

terms of 10-thousand work increments and break each chapter into roughly equal lengths. Here are some general guiding principles:

- 10,000 words = a pamphlet or business white paper. Read time = 30-60 minutes.
- 20,000 words = short eBook or manifesto. The Communist Manifesto is an example of this, at about 18,000 words. Read time = 1-2 hours.
- 40,000–60,000 words = standard nonfiction book / novella. The Great Gatsby is an example of this. Read time = three to four hours.
- 60,000–80,000 words = long nonfiction book / standard-length novel. Most Malcolm Gladwell books fit in this range. Read time = four to six hours.
- 80,000 words–100,000 words = very long nonfiction book / long novel. The Four-Hour Work Week falls in this range.
- 100,000+ words = epic-length novel / academic book / biography. Read time = six to eight hours. The Steve Jobs biography would fit this category.

6. Get early feedback ~ Have a few trusted advisers to help you discern what's worth writing. These can be friends, editors, family. Just try to find someone who will give you honest feedback early on to make sure you're headed in the right direction.

7. Embrace failure ~ As you approach the end of this project, know that this will be hard and you will most certainly mess up. Just be okay with failing, and give yourself grace.

8. Prepare for Publishing ~ It's time to decide how to publish, find an editor, and prepare for marketing.

Where Do I want My Books Sold Wish List"

_____
_____
_____
_____
_____
_____
_____
_____
_____
_____
_____
_____
_____

Who Do I want to Star In my Script?

_____
_____
_____
_____
_____
_____
_____
_____
_____
_____
_____
_____

Every Script has a Character, It's time to Audition Yours…

FINANCIAL GOALS

I WILL BUDGET WEEKLY/MONTHLY

Monthly income for the month of:
_____

Item	Amount
Salary	
Spouse's salary	
Dividends	
Interest	
Investments	
Reimbursements	
Other	
Total	

Monthly expenses for the month of:
_____

Item	Amount
Bills	
Groceries	
Mortgage	
Credit cards	
Gas	
IRA	
Laundry	
Car loan	
Utilities	
Clothing	
Daycare	
Medical/Dental	
Household repairs	
Savings	
Property taxes	

Other	
Total	

Income vs. Expenses

Item	Amount
Monthly income	
Monthly expenses	
Difference	

SAVING FOR A RAINY DAY PROVIDES STABILITY

I WILL BUDGET WEEKLY/MONTHLY

Monthly income for the month of:
_____

Item	Amount
Salary	
Spouse's salary	
Dividends	
Interest	
Investments	
Reimbursements	
Other	
Total	

Monthly expenses for the month of:
_____

Item	Amount
Bills	
Groceries	
Mortgage	
Credit cards	
Gas	
IRA	
Laundry	
Car loan	
Utilities	
Clothing	
Daycare	
Medical/Dental	
Household repairs	
Savings	
Property taxes	

Other	
Total	

Income vs. Expenses

Item	Amount
Monthly income	
Monthly expenses	
Difference	

SAVING FOR A RAINY DAY PROVIDES STABILITY

I WILL BUDGET WEEKLY/MONTHLY

Monthly income for the month of:
_____

Item	Amount
Salary	
Spouse's salary	
Dividends	
Interest	
Investments	
Reimbursements	
Other	
Total	

Monthly expenses for the month of:
_____

Item	Amount
Bills	
Groceries	
Mortgage	
Credit cards	
Gas	
IRA	
Laundry	
Car loan	
Utilities	
Clothing	
Daycare	
Medical/Dental	
Household repairs	
Savings	
Property taxes	

Other	
Total	

Income vs. Expenses

Item	Amount
Monthly income	
Monthly expenses	
Difference	

SAVING FOR A RAINY DAY PROVIDES STABILITY

I WILL BUDGET WEEKLY/MONTHLY

Monthly income for the month of:
_____

Item	Amount
Salary	
Spouse's salary	
Dividends	
Interest	
Investments	
Reimbursements	
Other	
Total	

Monthly expenses for the month of:
_____

Item	Amount
Bills	
Groceries	
Mortgage	
Credit cards	
Gas	
IRA	
Laundry	
Car loan	
Utilities	
Clothing	
Daycare	
Medical/Dental	
Household repairs	
Savings	
Property taxes	

Other	
Total	

Income vs. Expenses

Item	Amount
Monthly income	
Monthly expenses	
Difference	

SAVING FOR A RAINY DAY PROVIDES STABILITY

I WILL BUDGET WEEKLY/MONTHLY

Monthly income for the month of:
_____

Item	Amount
Salary	
Spouse's salary	
Dividends	
Interest	
Investments	
Reimbursements	
Other	
Total	

Monthly expenses for the month of:
_____

Item	Amount
Bills	
Groceries	
Mortgage	
Credit cards	
Gas	
IRA	
Laundry	
Car loan	
Utilities	
Clothing	
Daycare	
Medical/Dental	
Household repairs	
Savings	
Property taxes	

Other	
Total	

Income vs. Expenses

Item	**Amount**
Monthly income	
Monthly expenses	
Difference	

SAVING FOR A RAINY DAY PROVIDES STABILITY

I WILL BUDGET WEEKLY/MONTHLY

Monthly income for the month of:
_____

Item	Amount
Salary	
Spouse's salary	
Dividends	
Interest	
Investments	
Reimbursements	
Other	
Total	

Monthly expenses for the month of:
_____

Item	Amount
Bills	
Groceries	
Mortgage	
Credit cards	
Gas	
IRA	
Laundry	
Car loan	
Utilities	
Clothing	
Daycare	
Medical/Dental	
Household repairs	
Savings	
Property taxes	

Other	
Total	

Income vs. Expenses

Item	Amount
Monthly income	
Monthly expenses	
Difference	

SAVING FOR A RAINY DAY PROVIDES STABILITY

I WILL BUDGET WEEKLY/MONTHLY

Monthly income for the month of:
_____

Item	Amount
Salary	
Spouse's salary	
Dividends	
Interest	
Investments	
Reimbursements	
Other	
Total	

Monthly expenses for the month of:
_____

Item	Amount
Bills	
Groceries	
Mortgage	
Credit cards	
Gas	
IRA	
Laundry	
Car loan	
Utilities	
Clothing	
Daycare	
Medical/Dental	
Household repairs	
Savings	
Property taxes	

Other	
Total	

Income vs. Expenses

Item	Amount
Monthly income	
Monthly expenses	
Difference	

SAVING FOR A RAINY DAY PROVIDES STABILITY

I WILL BUDGET WEEKLY/MONTHLY

Monthly income for the month of:
_____

Item	Amount
Salary	
Spouse's salary	
Dividends	
Interest	
Investments	
Reimbursements	
Other	
Total	

Monthly expenses for the month of:
_____

Item	Amount
Bills	
Groceries	
Mortgage	
Credit cards	
Gas	
IRA	
Laundry	
Car loan	
Utilities	
Clothing	
Daycare	
Medical/Dental	
Household repairs	
Savings	
Property taxes	

Other	
Total	

Income vs. Expenses

Item	Amount
Monthly income	
Monthly expenses	
Difference	

SAVING FOR A RAINY DAY PROVIDES STABILITY

I WILL BUDGET WEEKLY/MONTHLY

Monthly income for the month of:
_____

Item	Amount
Salary	
Spouse's salary	
Dividends	
Interest	
Investments	
Reimbursements	
Other	
Total	

Monthly expenses for the month of:
_____

Item	Amount
Bills	
Groceries	
Mortgage	
Credit cards	
Gas	
IRA	
Laundry	
Car loan	
Utilities	
Clothing	
Daycare	
Medical/Dental	
Household repairs	
Savings	
Property taxes	

Other	
Total	

Income vs. Expenses

Item	Amount
Monthly income	
Monthly expenses	
Difference	

SAVING FOR A RAINY DAY PROVIDES STABILITY

I WILL BUDGET WEEKLY/MONTHLY

Monthly income for the month of:
_____

Item	Amount
Salary	
Spouse's salary	
Dividends	
Interest	
Investments	
Reimbursements	
Other	
Total	

Monthly expenses for the month of:
_____

Item	Amount
Bills	
Groceries	
Mortgage	
Credit cards	
Gas	
IRA	
Laundry	
Car loan	
Utilities	
Clothing	
Daycare	
Medical/Dental	
Household repairs	
Savings	
Property taxes	

Other	
Total	

Income vs. Expenses

Item	Amount
Monthly income	
Monthly expenses	
Difference	

SAVING FOR A RAINY DAY PROVIDES STABILITY

I WILL BUDGET WEEKLY/MONTHLY

Monthly income for the month of:
_____

Item	Amount
Salary	
Spouse's salary	
Dividends	
Interest	
Investments	
Reimbursements	
Other	
Total	

Monthly expenses for the month of:
_____

Item	Amount
Bills	
Groceries	
Mortgage	
Credit cards	
Gas	
IRA	
Laundry	
Car loan	
Utilities	
Clothing	
Daycare	
Medical/Dental	
Household repairs	
Savings	
Property taxes	

Other	
Total	

Income vs. Expenses

Item	Amount
Monthly income	
Monthly expenses	
Difference	

SAVING FOR A RAINY DAY PROVIDES STABILITY

I WILL BUDGET WEEKLY/MONTHLY

Monthly income for the month of:
_____

Item	Amount
Salary	
Spouse's salary	
Dividends	
Interest	
Investments	
Reimbursements	
Other	
Total	

Monthly expenses for the month of:
_____

Item	Amount
Bills	
Groceries	
Mortgage	
Credit cards	
Gas	
IRA	
Laundry	
Car loan	
Utilities	
Clothing	
Daycare	
Medical/Dental	
Household repairs	
Savings	
Property taxes	

Other	
Total	

Income vs. Expenses

Item	Amount
Monthly income	
Monthly expenses	
Difference	

SAVING FOR A RAINY DAY PROVIDES STABILITY

OPEN AN SAVINGS ACCOUNT

HAVE $1,000.00 IN AN EMERGENCY FUND

SAVE AT LEAST 10% OF YOUR MONTHLY EARNINGS

NICOLE LAPIN'S INCOME ALLOCATION ADVICE

70% for your basics of living utilities and transportation

10% for your Savings Account

15% for Retirement (investing)

Leaving: 5% of your monthly income for YOU

NEGOTIATE YOUR INTEREST RATES

Who says you can't negotiate credit card rates?

You can and should— especially if your interest rate is higher than average. Call and remind them of your punctuality and how loyal you've been, then hint that you're thinking of closing your card due to high interest. Some places will lower the rate to keep you.

The fed funds rate is the interest rate at which depository institutions (banks and credit unions) lend reserve balances to other depository institutions overnight, on an uncollateralized basis. ...

The current federal funds rate is 1.16%.

Tax Tips for Individuals

By Khristina Barnes, MSAC

Tax Professional & Owner of KMB Tax Service

- Examine the amount off federal and state withholdings that is being deducted from your paycheck. You can always contact a tax professional to help you determine whether the amount withheld is too low.

- Contribute to a retirement plan such as a 401k, Traditional IRA, Roth IRA, etc. Investing the maximum allowable contribution is a great way to reduce your taxable income.

- Educational plans, such as a 529 savings plan. When used for qualified educational expenses, earnings are not subject to federal tax and are general not subjected to state tax either.

- Healthcare savings plan, such as Health Savings Account (HSA). You can claim a tax deduction for the contributions you or someone other than your employer makes to your HSA account. There are several other benefits to having an HSA.

- Purchasing a home? Pay your property tax bill early. Even though real estate taxes may not be due until next year, you can pay them early and write off the entire expense this year. The IRS doesn't penalize you if you pay your property taxes early, and it allows you to take the entire tax deduction whether you pay early or on time.

- Purchase energy efficient upgrades to your home. As an incentive to conserve energy at home, the federal government offers tax credits to homeowners who purchase energy-saving improvements.

- Looking for a new job? Job search expenses such as job placement agency fees, mailing off resume's etc. You usually deduct your job search expenses on Schedule A, Itemized Deductions. You'll claim them as a miscellaneous deduction. You can deduct the total miscellaneous deductions that are more than two percent of your adjusted gross income.

- Donate to charitable organizations. You may deduct charitable contributions of money or property made to qualified organizations if you itemize your deductions. Generally, you may deduct up to 50 percent of your adjusted gross income, but 20 percent and 30 percent limitations apply in some cases.

INVESTING TYPES

Bonds. ...
Stocks. ...
Investment Funds. ...
Annuities. ...
Saving for College. ...
Retirement. ...

MY FINANCIAL GOALS ARE...

I PLAN TO ELIMINATE THESE CREDIT CARDS

My Investment Fear Is...

PROFESS YOUR CONNECTION WITH MONEY

I AM <u>A MONEY MAGNET</u>

I AM <u>ONE DOLLAR WAY FROM BEING A MILLIONAIRE</u>

I AM _____

_____

I AM _____

_____

I AM _____

_____

I AM _____

_____

I AM _____

_____

TIME TO TAKE A VACATION

ALL WORK AND NO PLAY, WILL MAKE FOR A GRUMPY PERSON.

USE THIS TIME TO LOOK BACK ON HOW MUCH YOU'VE ACCOMPLISHED

REFLECT, AND ENJOY THE CLARITY!

SO PROUD OF YOUR SUCCESS THUS FAR!

CHEERS !!!

BEFORE YOU MOVE FORWARD, USE THIS SPACE TO WRITE YOUR ACCOMPLISHMENTS, YOUR LESSONS LEARNED, AND EVERYTHING YOU HAVE IMPLEMENTED!

LIFESTYLE UPGRADES

WHERE AM I RIGHT NOW IN MY LIFE?

WHERE DO I WANT TO BE?

WHAT DO I WANT TO OWN?

HOW CAN I UPGRADE ME?

I HAVE A PASSPORT & WILL TO TRAVEL TO THESE COUNTRIES.

I NEED TO GET A PASSPORT SO I CAN TRAVEL TO THESE PLACES...

I WANT A MAKEOVER. I WILL CHANGE THESE THINGS ABOUT ME

(STYLE, HAIR, IMAGE)

_____
_____
_____
_____
_____
_____
_____
_____
_____
_____
_____
_____
_____
_____
_____
_____
_____
_____
_____
_____
_____
_____
_____

TRACK YOUR HOMEBUYER PROCESS

I AM READY TO PURCHASE TO A HOME

Step 1: Check Your Credit Report & Score.
Step 2: Figure out How Much You Can Afford.
Step 3: Find the Right Lender and Real Estate Agent.
Step 4: Look for the Right Home.
Step 5: Make an Offer on the Home.
Step 6: Get the Right Mortgage for Your Situation.
Step 7: Close on Your Home.
Step 8: Move In!

NOW TAKE EACH HOME OWNERSHIP STEP AND GIVE YOURSELF A DEADLINE.

STEP 1

STEP 2

STEP 3

STEP 4

STEP 5

STEP 6

STEP 7

STEP 8

I WILL UPDATE MY RESUME

(paste your resume here)

I WILL APPLY FOR THESE EXTRA CLASSES TO STRENGTHEN MY SKILLS

I OWE IT TO MYSELF TO ACHIEVE THESE THINGS TO ELEVATE MYSELF

1. _____

2. _____

3. _____

4. _____

5. _____

6. _____

7. _____

FITNESS GOALS

HEALTH IS WEALTH. AM I LIVING A HEALTHY LIFESTYLE?

(Write Health Goals)

1. _____

2. _____

3. _____

4. _____

5. _____

6. _____

7. _____

EXERCISE DAILY

Exercise 1: Bodyweight Squat
Stand as tall as you can with your feet spread slightly wider than shoulder-width apart. Hold your arms straight out in front of your body at shoulder level, so that your arms parallel to the floor. Keep your torso as upright as you can for the entire movement, with your lower back slightly arched. Brace your abs, and lower your body as far as you can by pushing your hips back and bending your knees. Pause, then push yourself back to the starting position. That's one repetition. Do 15 to 20 repetitions.

Exercise 2: Incline Push-up
Assume a push-up position, but place your hands placed on a raised surface—such as a box, bench, ottoman or one of the steps of your stairs—instead of the floor. Your body should form a straight line from your ankles to your head. Keeping your body rigid, lower your body until your upper arms dip below your elbows. Pause, and then push yourself back to the starting position as quickly as possible. (The higher the surface on which you place your hands, the easier the exercise becomes—you can even lean against a wall if you need to.) If the incline push-up is too easy, do it the old-fashioned way, with your hands on the floor. Do 12 to 15 repetitions.

Exercise 3: Hip Raise
Lie on your back on the floor with your knees bent and your feet flat on the floor. Place your arms out to your sides at a 45-degree angle, your palms facing up. Now try to make your tummy as skinny as possible and hold it that way—this gives you a tight core—while breathing normally. That's the starting position. Keeping your core tight, squeeze your glutes and raise your hips so your body forms a straight line from your shoulders to your knees. Pause for five seconds—squeezing your glutes tightly the entire time—then lower body back to the starting position. Do 10 repetitions.

Exercise 4: Side Plank
Lie on your right side with your knees straight. Prop your upper body on your right elbow and forearm, which should be directly below your right shoulder. Place your left hand on your left hip. Try to make your tummy as skinny as possible and hold it that way—this gives you a tight core—while breathing normally. Then raise your hips until your body forms a straight line from your ankles to your shoulders. With your core tight, hold this position for 30 seconds. Roll onto your other side and repeat.

Modified Side Plank
If the side plank is too difficult, hold for five seconds, rest for five seconds, and repeat as many times as needed to total 30 seconds. Each time you perform the exercise, try to hold each repetition a little longer, so that you reach your 30-second goal with fewer repetitions. If that's still too hard, bend your knees 90 degrees and allow your lower legs to rest on the floor as you do the exercise. (Your body will now form a straight line from your knees to your shoulders.)

Exercise 5: Floor Y-T-I Raises
This is a three-exercise combination move. You'll simply perform 8 to 12 repetitions of each exercise, one after the other without resting. So do 8 to 12 reps of the Floor Y raise, followed immediately by 8 to 12 reps of the Floor T raise, followed immediately by 8 to 12 reps of the Floor I raise.

Floor Y Raise
Lie face down on the floor with your arms resting on the floor, completely straight and at a 30-degree angle to your body, so they form a "Y." Your palms should be facing each other, so that the thumb side of your hand points up.

FITNESS TIPS

By Personal Fitness Professional Kenneth Nelson Jr.

Owner of FitZonFit at Phit Club Fitness Club

Exercise Physiologist /Certified Master Fitness Trainer

Fitness Tip #1: Form is everything! If your form is off, you are bound for injuries.

Fitness Tip #2: Portion Control is the key to Weight Loss. Servings shouldn't be more than the palm of your hand.

Fitness Tip #3: Muscle Burns Fat! Strength Train! You don't have to lift heavy, you just have lift consistently...

Fitness Tip #4: Fitness has 4 components: Strength, Endurance, Balance, and Flexibility

Fitness Tip #5: Speed is only accomplished through proper technique. The better the technique the faster you will become.

Fitness Tip #6: Cardio regulates the density of your body fat, but you need Strength Training to keep the density down.

Fitness Tip #7: The Body requires 3 nutrients: Carbohydrates, Fats and Proteins... The Body needs Carbs for Energy... Fats for Warmth... Proteins for Recovery and Repair

- Carbs ~ Complex- Breads, Pastas, Starches
- Simple ~ Fruits and Veggies
- Fats ~ Nuts, Dairy
- Proteins ~ Meats and Beans

Fitness Tip #8: In order to reach your fitness goals you need to embrace the process...

There is NO PROGRESS without PROCESS...

I WILL JOIN A GYM TODAY.

(PASTE YOUR GYM MEMBERSHIP RECIPT HERE)

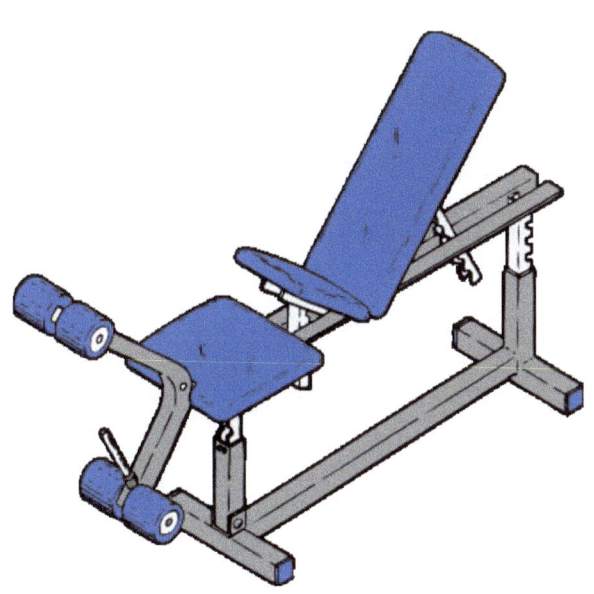

I WILL EAT HEALTHER

You should base your diet on these real, unprocessed.

- **Meat:** Beef, lamb, pork, chicken and others. Grass-fed is best.
- **Fish:** Salmon, trout, haddock and many others. Wild-caught fish is best.
- **Eggs:** Omega-3 enriched or pastured eggs are best.
- **Vegetables:** Spinach, broccoli, cauliflower, carrots.
- **Fruits:** Apples, oranges, pears, blueberries, strawberries.
- **Nuts and Seeds:** Almonds, walnuts, sunflower seeds, etc.
- **High-Fat Dairy:** Cheese, butter, heavy cream, yogurt.
- **Fats and Oils:** Coconut oil, butter, lard, olive oil and cod fish liver oil.

A Sample Menu For One Week

This is a sample menu for one week on a low carb diet plan. It provides less than 50 grams of total carbs per day, but if you are healthy and active you can go beyond that.

Monday

- **Breakfast:** Omelet with various vegetables, fried in butter or coconut oil.
- **Lunch:** Grass-fed yogurt with blueberries and a handful of almonds.
- **Dinner:** Cheeseburger (no bun), served with vegetables and salsa sauce.

Tuesday

- **Breakfast:** Bacon and eggs.
- **Lunch:** Leftover burgers and veggies from the night before.

- **Dinner:** Salmon with butter and vegetables.

Wednesday

- **Breakfast:** Eggs and vegetables, fried in butter or coconut oil.
- **Lunch:** Shrimp salad with some olive oil.
- **Dinner:** Grilled chicken with vegetables.

Thursday

- **Breakfast:** Omelet with various vegetables, fried in butter or coconut oil.
- **Lunch:** Smoothie with coconut milk, berries, almonds and protein powder.
- **Dinner:** Steak and veggies.

Friday

- **Breakfast:** Bacon and Eggs.
- **Lunch:** Chicken salad with some olive oil.
- **Dinner:** Pork chops with vegetables.

Saturday

- **Breakfast:** Omelet with various veggies.
- **Lunch:** Grass-fed yogurt with berries, coconut flakes and a handful of walnuts.
- **Dinner:** Meatballs with vegetables.

Sunday

- **Breakfast:** Bacon and Eggs.
- **Lunch:** Smoothie with coconut milk, a bit of heavy cream, chocolate-flavored protein powder and berries.

- **Dinner:** Grilled chicken wings with some raw spinach on the side.

Include plenty of low-carb vegetables in your diet. If your goal is to remain under 50 grams of carbs per day, then there is room for plenty of veggies and one fruit per day.

Some Healthy, Low-Carb Snacks

There is no health reason to eat more than 3 meals per day, but if you get hungry between meals then here are some healthy, easy to prepare snacks that can fill you up:

- A Piece of Fruit
- Full-fat Yogurt
- A Hard-Boiled Egg or Two
- Baby Carrots
- Leftovers From The Night Before
- A Handful of Nuts
- Some Cheese and Meat

Foods to Avoid

You should avoid these 7 foods, in order of importance:

- **Sugar:** Soft drinks, fruit juices, agave, candy, ice cream and many others.

- **Trans Fats:** "Hydrogenated" or "partially hydrogenated" oils.

- **High Omega-6 Seed- and Vegetable Oils:** Cottonseed-, soybean-, sunflower-, grapeseed-, corn-, safflower and canola oils.

- **Artificial Sweeteners:** Aspartame, Saccharin, Sucralose, Cyclamates and Acesulfame Potassium. Use Stevia instead.

- **Highly Processed Foods:** If it looks like it was made in a factory, don't eat it.

- **White Bread:** White Bread is highly refined and often contains a lot of added sugar.

- **Pastries, Cookies and Cakes**: Pastries, cookies and cakes are packed with unhealthy ingredients like added sugar and refined flour.

- **Fried Foods:** Fried Foods are not good because of the oil intake. If you're going to eat fried foods, make them yourself at home, where you can use olive, soybean, and canola oils.

HOW DO I MEASURE?

Height and Weight Chart

Height	Weight Normal	Overweight
4' 10"	91 to 118 lbs.	119 to 142 lbs.
4' 11"	94 to 123 lbs.	124 to 147 lbs.
5'	97 to 127 lbs.	128 to 152 lbs.
5' 1"	100 to 131 lbs.	132 to 157 lbs.
5' 2"	104 to 135 lbs.	136 to 163 lbs.
5' 3"	107 to 140 lbs.	141 to 168 lbs.

5' 4"	110 to 144 lbs.	145 to 173 lbs.
5' 5"	114 to 149 lbs.	150 to 179 lbs.
5' 6"	118 to 154 lbs.	155 to 185 lbs.
5' 7"	121 to 158 lbs.	159 to 190 lbs.
5' 8"	125 to 163 lbs.	164 to 196 lbs.
5' 9"	128 to 168 lbs.	169 to 202 lbs.
5' 10"	132 to 173 lbs.	174 to 208 lbs.
5' 11"	136 to 178 lbs.	179 to 214 lbs.
6'	140 to 183 lbs.	184 to 220 lbs.
6' 1"	144 to 188 lbs.	189 to 226 lbs.

6' 2"	148 to 193 lbs.	194 to 232 lbs.
6' 3"	152 to 199 lbs.	200 to 239 lbs.
6' 4"	156 to 204 lbs.	205 to 245 lbs.

HAPPINESS & PEACE BELONGS TO MY FREEDOM

HAVING FREEDOM WILL ENABLE ME TO DO......

EVERYDAY I WILL BE HAPPY. I WILL ACHIEVE THIS BY...

WHEN I AM TRIED AND TESTED, I WILL DO THE FOLLOWING TO MAINTAIN MY PEACE …..

I HAVE TO REMOVE TOXIC PEOPLE.........

(List 8 people who you will love from a distance)

1. _____

2. _____

3. _____

4. _____

5. _____

6. _____

7. _____

8. _____

I WILL MEDIATE 20 MINUTES A DAY

I WILL TAKE ONE DAY A WEEK AND "TREAT" MYSELF.

I WILL TAKE ONE WEEKEND A MONTH AND DO NOTHING.

(Using the calendars in the beginning of the book, schedule one weekend a month for Yourself.)

I RESPECT MYSELF ENOUGH TO NOT DO THE FOLLOWING ...

GOOGLE AND FIND 1 EMPOWERMENT AND 1 FINANCIAL WORKSHOPS YOU WILL ATTEND.

(REGISTER AND MAKE SURE YOU WRITE THOSE EVENTS ON THIS PAGE AND ON YOUR CALENDAR)

PAY IT FORWARD. PURCHASE THIS JOURNAL FOR SOMEONE YOU KNOW THAT IS READY FOR A BETTER LIFE.

PURGE AND LET GO

(Go through your house and let go of everything you don't want, don't use, and don't need)

I AM THE HAPPIEST WHEN I AM..

AFFIRM HAPPINESS

I am a naturally happy person

Life just feels great all the time

I can easily pick myself up and lift my spirits when needed

Being optimistic comes easily to me

I am the one that others look to for reassurance during difficult times

Great things always seem to come my way

I feel a natural sense of peace and happiness within myself

Being happy all the time is normal for me

I choose to have a positive view of myself and others

I am filled with a sense of gratitude for being alive

AFFIRM PEACE

All is well.

I am in the right place at the right time.

I love my life.

My life is in perfect balance.

I will make the best decisions for my life.

I am surrounded by loving relationships.

I live my life with purpose.

I am safe and supported.

I am healthy and strong.

I love myself.

BROADEN MY HORIZON

BOOKS TO READ

NEW ADVENTURES TO TRY

MOVIES TO SEE

CONCERTS TO ATTEND

RESTAURANTS TO TRY

RECIPES TO TRY

PEOPLE I WANT TO CONNECT WITH....

ABOUT THE AUTHOR
CHARRON MONAYE

Like many young girls, Charron Monaye kept a journal, except hers consisted of poetry which she never expected to give a voice. Only out of necessity did she put it on paper. To hold it inside was too overwhelming. Finally releasing her thoughts, even if only on paper, was empowering.

That defining moment led to her becoming an Award-winning playwright/author/coach/entrepreneur and writer. After overcoming multiple panic attacks at the ripe young age of thirty, Charron had to learn how to give her pain a voice while not blaming herself in the midst. She had to remove toxicity, manage overwhelming financial setbacks, and muster up the strength to leave an unhealthy marriage, all while raising her children. In the midst of it all, Charron Monaye adapted a new sense of survival while being ready to open up about losing everything…and finding peace in the process.

To find her voice, power, and strength, she released her first book of poetry, "My Side of the Story," in 2010 under Purposeful Publishing, LLC. It was so raw, so transparent about her marriage and divorce, that it was adapted into a stage play entitled "Living Your Life" and featured in the Black Theater Festival in Washington D.C. with actress D'atra Hicks. Realizing the power of her words, Charron created her literacy company, Pen Legacy, in 2015, which offers self-publishing, script-writing and writing services, and writing/empowerment coaching. Since then, Charron Monaye have authored 8 books, co-authored 4, published over 25 new authors, written/produced 3 theatrical productions, contributed to more than 20 book anthologies worldwide, and hired to pen other theatrical scripts such as; Testify, Til Death Do us Part, Oliva Lost Turned Out, just to name a few. Charron was formerly a staff writer for the Philadelphia Association of Paralegals, CNN iReport, and currently serves as a staff writer for the Department of Veteran Affairs, GovLoop.com, and Editor-In-Chief for www.madisonjaye.com. And is preparing to produce her first film, which started out as a book and later adapted into a theatrical production, "Get Out Of Your Own Way". In 2017, she received a Doctorate of Philosophy (Humane Letters) from CICA International University Seminary. Just recently, she had the opportunity to hone her writing skills by studying under television producer, screenwriter, and author Shonda Rhimes and NAACP Image Award Author Victoria Christopher Murray. Charron has a Bachelor's of Arts in Political Science from West Chester University, Master's in Public Administration from Keller Graduate School of Management, a Certificate in Paralegal Studies and Life Coaching. Charron is an active member of Zeta Phi Beta Sorority, Incorporated and Order of Eastern Star.

Contact Info:
Author Website: www.Charron Monaye .com
Email: info@penlegacy.com
Business Website: www.penlegacy.com
Facebook Twitter: PenLegacy
Instagram: iamcharronmonaye
LinkedIn: Charron Monaye , MPA

Books Published By Pen Legacy Publishing

Journals/Guides

Boss Moves Start With You: 2018 Self-Reflection Journal Vision Planner by: Briana McKnight

Maximizing Your Tax Refund Made Easy! by: Khristina Barnes

Book Anthologies

Bruised, Broken, and Blessed: Life Changing Stories That Will Ignite Hope, Elevate Personal Growth, and Confirm Your Greatness compiled by Charron Monaye & Shontaye Hawkins

Get Out Of Your Own Way: Overcoming Adversity to Live In Your Truth Out Loud compiled by Charron Monaye

Inspirational/Non-Fiction

Respect Your Choices: Finding Balance in Success by: Vaughn McNeill

Let Me Tell You Like I Told Myself: Love's Truth Never Changes by: Summer Willow Fitch

The Power of Shut Up by: Lisa Dove Washington

Christian Fiction

MisLeading Lady by: Sharon Y. Judie

Parenting/Caregiver

Shattering The Barriers of Single Motherhood: A Single Mom's guide to Power, Resilience, and the Pursuit of Happiness by: Sang Thi Duong

From CAREFREE to CAREGIVER: A 31 Devotional to Balance, Encourage, and Support You in Your New Role by: Teraleen Campbell

Fiction

Leonard Smith by: AJ Harrison

Memoirs

The Black Blood In My Heart by: La'Mena Marie

The Shadow In My Eyes by Deborah Rose

The Woodshed by Jaguar Wright

How I Survived Without Chemo Therapy: One Woman's Story From Diagnosed To Thriving by Sabrina Moore

Stop Being a Doormat & Start Being a Boss by Toni Moore

> Books are available on Amazon, Barnes N Noble, Books A Million, Wal-Mart,
> Penlegacy.com

www.ingramcontent.com/pod-product-compliance
Ingram Content Group UK Ltd.
Pitfield, Milton Keynes, MK11 3LW, UK
UKHW020719050526
12271UKWH00018B/222